Earth-Friendly Buildings

Miriam Coleman

WITHDRAWN

PowerKiDS press

New York

Published in 2011 by The Rosen Publishing Group, Inc.
29 East 21st Street, New York, NY 10010

First Edition

Editor: Joanne Randolph
Book Design: Kate Laczynski

Photo Credits: Cover, p. 25 Dan Kitwood/Getty Images; p. 4 Jupiterimages/Comstock/Thinkstock; pp. 5, 6, 14, 16, 22 iStockphoto/Thinkstock; p. 7 Stockbyte/Thinkstock; pp. 8–9 Sean Gallup/Getty Images; p. 10 Business Wire/Getty Images; p. 11 Andy Nelson/The Christian Science Monitor/Getty Images; pp. 12–13 Andreas Rentz/Getty Images; p. 15 Romeo Gacad/AFP/Getty Images; p. 17 Jim Watson/AFP/Getty Images; p. 18 © www.iStockphoto.com/Katy Hollbacher; p. 19 Jupiterimages/Brand X Pictures/Thinkstock; pp. 20–21 Robert Nickelsberg/Getty Images; p. 23 David Sacks/Lifesize/Thinkstock; p. 24 (top) Jupiterimages/Photos.com/Thinkstock; p. 24 (bottom) Jupiterimages/Creatas/Thinkstock; pp. 26–27 Michael S. Yamashita/Getty Images; p. 28 Washington Post/Getty Images; p. 29 Universal Images Group/Getty Images; p. 30 Eco Images/Universal Images Group/Getty Images.

Library of Congress Cataloging-in-Publication Data

Coleman, Miriam.
 Earth-friendly buildings / by Miriam Coleman. — 1st. ed.
      p. cm. — (How to be Earth friendly)
Includes index.
ISBN 978-1-4488-2588-2 (library binding) — ISBN 978-1-4488-2765-7 (pbk.) — ISBN 978-1-4488-2766-4 (6-pack)
1. Sustainable architecture—Juvenile literature. I. Title.
NA2542.36.C63 2011
720'.47—dc22
                              2010034464

Manufactured in the United States of America

CPSIA Compliance Information: Batch #WW11PK: For Further Information contact Rosen Publishing, New York, New York at 1-800-237-9932

CONTENTS

What Is an Earth-Friendly Building?

The human population is growing. There are more people living on our planet than there were in the past. All these people need places to live and work. To meet these people's needs, we build more homes and offices.

As we create new buildings, however, we must think of the future. This way Earth can continue to support all the people who will live on it. To construct and run buildings, we

Here a new building is under construction. Construction sites are messy and loud. Sometimes they also create a lot of waste that is not good for Earth.

IT'S A FACT!

The LEED system is used to measure how green a building is. "LEED" stands for "Leadership in Energy and Environmental Design." The highest LEED rating is platinum.

need **resources**. We can build in a way that uses resources wisely, though. This Earth-friendly way of building is called **sustainable architecture**, or green building.

Earth-friendly building has several purposes. It aims to cause as little harm to the natural **environment** as possible. It also tries

The Hearst Building, shown here, is the first green building in New York City. It is rated gold by the LEED system, which is just under platinum, the highest rating.

5

Perlan, a building in Iceland, is heated using geothermal energy from deep inside Earth. After the building was completed, 176,000 trees were planted on the land around it.

to use resources, such as water and energy, **efficiently**. Green building works to keep the people who live and work in buildings healthy by reducing harmful chemicals in building **materials**. It also reduces the amount of waste and pollution that buildings create.

Why Build Earth Friendly?

When lots of people and cars crowd together in cities, it can cause smog like what you can see here. Smog is not healthy to breathe.

More than a million single-family homes are built in the United States every year. Combined with all the offices and other buildings we build, this has a huge impact on the environment.

Conventional building practices have been careless about the resources that are used in building. Huge areas

7

of land are cleared of native plants and animals to make way for new homes. Forests are cut down to provide wood. Buildings are poorly constructed so that heating and cooling take far more energy than needed. Poor-quality materials need to be replaced often. We paint, clean, and put buildings together with materials that have **toxic** chemicals in them. This is not good for us or for the environment.

These smokestacks let out steam from a coal-fired power plant. This plant gives people power for lights, heat, and cooking. It is hurting the environment, too, though.

Due to all this carelessness, buildings in the United States account for nearly 40 percent of the nation's total **carbon dioxide** emissions. These gases contribute to environmental problems such as pollution and **global warming**.

Earth-friendly building practices cause fewer problems for the environment and produce less waste. Earth-friendly building can also save people and businesses money by reducing energy bills.

Growing Communities, Building Smart

Where you build a home or office can be just as important for the environment as how you build it. If you build near schools, stores, work, and public

A company in Denver, Colorado, builds Earth-friendly apartment buildings in the city. It uses sustainable materials and wind power provides the electricity.

transportation, people will not have to drive cars as often to get where they need to go. This helps reduce fuel use and air pollution. Creating new homes and buildings in areas close to the resources people need is called smart growth or sustainable development.

Once builders have chosen the place where the new home or office will go, they need to look at how they treat the land on which they will build. Instead of clearing out all the trees and plants from the lot, it is best to

IT'S A FACT!

In 2002, the amount of land occupied by cities was four times what it was in 1945. That means that a lot of farmland, forests, and wetlands were covered, cut down, or filled in during that time. This means a great number of plants and animals were lost.

The Sidwell Friends School in Washington, D.C., has a building with a LEED platinum rating. It was built with recycled and local materials. It also uses solar and wind power and has a green roof.

leave as many as possible where they are. The trees can provide shade to cool the building in the summer. They can also shelter a building against cold winds in the winter.

Building a smaller house means you can leave more trees and plants on

Do you see the blue strips along the side of this apartment building? They are solar panels used to make electricity for the people living there.

the land. A smaller house uses fewer resources because you need less furniture to fill it. There is also not as much space to clean. It takes less energy to heat and cool a smaller house, too.

It takes a lot of water and a lot of fuel for mowing to keep grassy lawns looking green and tidy. Local plants that are suited to your climate will not need as much extra water or food.

Cutting Down on Waste

Dump trucks must drive the waste from a construction site to a landfill to dump it. This not only fills up landfills, but the trucks also burn gas and dirty the air.

If you have ever watched workers building a house, you likely saw trucks taking away huge amounts of waste materials, such as wood trimmings, concrete, and metal. Have you ever wondered where all that waste goes? It often goes into landfills, which are areas where garbage

The construction of an average 2,000-square-foot (186 sq m) house can create more than 1 ton (1 t) of construction waste!

is buried underground. Sometimes the garbage lets out harmful chemicals into the earth.

Earth-friendly builders are careful about the waste they produce. They recycle any materials that can be used again on other buildings. Earth-friendly builders also try hard not to create a lot of waste. They measure and cut things carefully so that

This forest in Indonesia is being cleared by a company that makes palm oil. Indonesia has some of the highest carbon dioxide emissions in the world.

15

IT'S A FACT!

Another way builders try to save energy is by using local materials. This saves the fuel that would otherwise be used in trucking something from farther away.

Green builders try to find materials, such as stone and wood, from local places. It costs a lot of money to ship materials such as Italian marble, shown here, by plane.

they have few trimmings to throw away. They also try to build with materials that will last a long time, so that parts do not need to be thrown away and replaced too often. Finally, they try to use safe materials so that when they do end up in landfills, they will not poison the earth.

Earth-Friendly Building Materials

This insulation is made from recycled clothing. It does not cost much and is great at keeping houses from getting too hot or cold.

Constructing a new building requires a lot of materials and resources. Using a lot of nonrenewable resources can hurt the environment. If large amounts of a renewable resource are taken from one place, this can hurt the environment, too. An average-size house in the United States uses the wood of up to 44 trees, or 1 acre (.4 ha) of land!

Cork trees grow thick bark. It can be taken off the tree every 9 to 12 years without hurting the tree. Sustainable builders may choose to use floors made from cork.

One way to build green is by choosing materials wisely. Rather than using new wood taken from an **endangered** rain forest in South America, many people today choose to recycle wood from other buildings. For example, a staircase can be made from the wooden boards of an old barn.

Builders have long used a material called fiberglass to provide **insulation** for homes. Fiberglass takes a lot of

This man is holding a compact fluorescent lightbulb, or CFL. Using CFLs in your home can save your parents money and help save Earth!

You can make a big difference in making your home Earth friendly just by changing a lightbulb! Conventional lightbulbs, called incandescent bulbs, last only about 1,000 hours. Compact fluorescent lightbulbs use much less energy and can last 10,000 hours.

energy to produce. It often uses toxic chemicals as well. Earth-friendly builders look for other kinds of insulation, such as recycled denim. This kind of insulation is made from scraps of jeans and other cotton cloth. You can even recycle the recycled denim insulation when it gets too old!

Making Your Own Energy

It takes a lot of energy to run a building. In fact, 70 percent of all electricity produced in the United States goes into powering buildings. Lighting, heating, and cooling rooms and heating water all use electricity. Most of the electricity comes from far-away power plants that burn coal and natural gas. These plants cause

These workers are putting solar panels on the roof of a school in Pleasanton, California. Seven schools in this town decided to help Earth by using solar power.

air pollution. They also add to global warming. What if a house could make its own energy, though?

Many Earth-friendly buildings today use **solar panels** to capture energy from the Sun. This energy is turned into electricity. Some homes, businesses, or towns may also use wind power to create electricity.

IT'S A FACT!

Aside from making your own energy, proper insulation is one of the most important ways to reduce your energy bill. Gaps and cracks in a house's roof or walls can waste 30 percent of the energy you use to keep it warm or cool.

You can take advantage of the Sun's energy even without solar panels. The Sun shines brightest on the south side of a house. Putting living rooms in that part of the house makes the most of the daytime light. It saves electricity and the costs of heating those rooms are lower, too!

Some homes, such as this one, may decide to use a wind turbine to make electricity for their daily activities.

Monument Valley Regional Middle School, in Great Barrington, Massachusetts, uses 88 solar panels to produce more than 13 percent of its own electricity. The school also uses **geothermal energy**, which is the power of the natural heat at Earth's core. Pipes beneath the school heat water deep under ground. Then the pipes move the hot water throughout the school to heat the classrooms.

Lowering VOCs

When we think about poor air quality, we often imagine smog caused by the pollution coming from cars and factories. The level of air pollution inside buildings is often two to five times worse than outside, though!

Keeping the air inside buildings safe is an important part of Earth-friendly building. One source of poor indoor air quality comes from the paint on the walls. In the past, paint had large amounts of volatile organic compounds, or VOCs.

Choosing paints that are low in VOCs is good for your family and the environment.

VOCs are chemicals that get into the air and cause health problems, such as breathing trouble, headaches, and skin and eye **irritations**. Today, you can buy paint with low amounts of VOCs.

Cabinets made from plywood can be sources of VOCs, too. Thin sheets of wood are glued together to make plywood. The glue can have VOCs, such as formaldehyde, in them. Earth-friendly builders can build cabinets from a plywood **substitute** made from wheat straw instead.

Check labels carefully to make sure the products you buy are made using things that come from nature.

Green Roofs and Rain Gardens

At the Ballard Library, in Seattle, a garden of wild thyme, grass, and other plants grows on the roof. It may seem strange to have a garden growing right on top of a library. The plants are very helpful to both the building and the environment around it.

These green roofs are not only being used to grow plants, but people are raising bees on them, too. Bees help plants grow, so this rooftop is helping Earth in two ways!

A roof that is covered in plants is called a green roof. Green roofs benefit buildings and their surroundings in many different ways. In heavy rain, the water usually runs off regular roofs and collects in storm sewers. If there is too much rain, the storm drains overflow and let harmful

Even if you cannot have a green roof, growing some potted plants on the roof helps. Those plants catch and hold rain. They also help make better air for people to breathe.

chemicals into local rivers. Green roofs absorb much of that rain and use it to feed the plants.

The plants that grow on green roofs do many wonderful things. Like all plants, they turn carbon dioxide into oxygen. This improves air quality and fights global warming. They also

provide homes for insects and birds. They even provide insulation, which helps keep buildings warm in the winter and cool in the summer.

If you cannot plant a garden on your roof, you can still fight storm water pollution with a rain garden. Rain gardens allow water to

Modern green roofs use systems of layers to protect the buildings from water and plant roots. Green roofs are really an ancient idea, however. The Vikings covered their houses with pieces of grass called sod.

soak into your yard and feed plants instead of running into the street. A bowl-shaped dip in the garden directs the water toward the plants. Rain gardens use plants with sturdy roots that are better at absorbing water than ordinary lawn grass.

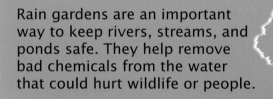

Rain gardens are an important way to keep rivers, streams, and ponds safe. They help remove bad chemicals from the water that could hurt wildlife or people.

The Future of Earth-Friendly Building

This is a sustainable home set into the ground in Wales. Setting a home into the ground helps keep it from getting too hot or cold.

Earth-friendly building is on the rise. Some people believe that 10 years from now, all new buildings will be green. Energy costs keep going up and Earth-friendly technologies have become more widespread and less expensive. Therefore, more people are choosing a sustainable way of life.

The next step in Earth-friendly building is the living building. Instead of just using less energy and fewer

The Omega Center for Sustainable Living, in Rhinebeck, New York, is an example of a living building. It uses geothermal heating, solar panels, and rain gardens.

This sustainable home has solar panels and a green roof. It was built with natural, local materials, too.

resources, living buildings aim to use no more energy than they create themselves. Some living buildings may actually make enough electricity to power other buildings!

You do not need to build a whole new house to practice Earth-friendly building, however. In fact, it's even better to make do with what you have for as long as you can. Small steps, such as using low-VOC paint and fixing leaks in your home, can make a huge difference.

GLOSSARY

carbon dioxide (KAR-bin dy-OK-syd) An odorless, colorless gas. People breathe out carbon dioxide.

conventional (kun-VENCH-nul) Generally accepted.

efficiently (ih-FIH-shent-lee) Done in the quickest, best way possible.

endangered (in-DAYN-jerd) In danger of no longer existing.

environment (en-VY-ern-ment) Everything that surrounds human beings and other living things and everything that makes it possible for them to live.

geothermal energy (JEE-oh-ther-mul EH-ner-jee) Power that is made using the heat at Earth's core.

global warming (GLOH-bul WAWRM-ing) A gradual increase in how hot Earth is. It is caused by gases that are let out when people burn fuels such as gasoline.

insulation (in-suh-LAY-shun) Matter that covers something and stops heat or sound from flowing out of it.

irritations (ir-uh-TAY-shunz) Pains or discomforts.

materials (muh-TEER-ee-ulz) What things are made of.

resources (REE-sawrs-ez) Supplies or sources of energy or useful things.

solar panels (SOH-ler PA-nulz) Collectors to capture and store solar energy.

substitute (SUB-stuh-toot) Something used in place of something else.

sustainable architecture (suh-STAY-nuh-bel AHR-kuh-tek-chur) Building using renewable resources, or resources that cannot be used up and do not harm our planet.

toxic (TOK-sik) Poisonous.

transportation (tranz-per-TAY-shun) A way of traveling from one place to another.

INDEX

WEB SITES

Due to the changing nature of Internet links, PowerKids Press has developed an online list of Web sites related to the subject of this book. This site is updated regularly. Please use this link to access the list:
www.powerkidslinks.com/hbef/building/